Telephones Are Better Than Men Because...
Or, What Women Would Say If They Dared

KAREN ROSTOKER-GRUBER

Illustrations by Don Smith

LONGSTREET PRESS
Atlanta, Georgia

Published by LONGSTREET PRESS, INC.,
a subsidiary of Cox Newspapers,
a subsidiary of Cox Enterprises, Inc.
2140 Newmarket Parkway
Suite 118
Marietta, Georgia 30067

Copyright © 1996 by Karen Rostoker-Gruber
Illustrations copyright © 1996 by Don Smith

Printed in the United States of America

1st printing, 1996

Library of Congress Catalog Number 96-76740

ISBN: 1-56352-343-4

This book was printed by United Graphics, Inc., Mattoon, Il

Cover illustration and design by Rhino Graphics
Book design by Jill Dible

This book is dedicated to John Yow, Marge McDonald, and Ruth Waters, who always go that extra mile for me; to my husband, Scott; and to Jean Marie Day and Gail Panzer-Salmanowitz, who listened to countless revisions of this book with a smile.

Telephones Are Better Than Men Because...

almost every bedroom has one waiting.

Telephones Are Better Than Men Because…

you can screw them to the wall.

you can adjust their tone.

they don't drive at warp speed to impress you.

1

Telephones Are Better Than Men Because ...

you can upgrade them.

they don't chew with their mouth open.

you can get one cheap with a company discount.

they don't come home smelling of cigar smoke.

they never say, "I only read *Playboy* for the articles."

Telephones Are Better Than Men Because...

you can replace their parts.

they don't stand you up (but you can stand them up).

they don't mind if you brag about their quick performance to your friends.

Telephones Are Better Than Men Because ...

they don't expect you to cook for them.

Telephones Are Better Than Men Because...

they have a hold button.

they don't brag about how big their base unit is.

you can hold them with one hand and drive with the other.

Telephones Are Better Than Men Because...

you can turn them off as easily as you can turn them on.

you know how to push all the right buttons.

you can use them in front of your friends.

 8

Telephones Are Better Than Men Because...

once you've used one, you know how to use them all.

you can play with them on a plane.

they don't bring home a huge fish and expect you to gut it.

Telephones Are Better Than Men Because...

they don't have holes in their underwear.

Telephones Are Better Than Men Because ...

they don't mind meeting your parents.

Telephones Are Better Than Men Because ...

they don't compare you with other women
who have held them.

Telephones Are Better Than Men Because...

you can keep one in your pocket for convenience.

they don't buy tons of gadgets for their cars.

they never say, "I'll call you."

they don't screw up your phone messages.

Telephones Are Better Than Men Because...

you can touch them wherever you want and immediately get the desired result.

they don't adjust themselves in public.

they don't leave change lying around the house.

Telephones Are Better Than Men Because...

they don't get drunk.

you never have to worry about what they're doing.

you can share them with your friends.

Telephones Are Better Than Men Because...

technology can't improve men.

you don't have to wear lingerie to turn them on.

Telephones Are Better Than Men Because...

you can leave them at the office.

they don't whine like babies whenever
you take them shopping.

they don't have body odor.

Telephones Are Better Than Men Because...

they don't care if you have five closets full of clothes.

Telephones Are Better Than Men Because...

they don't try to take advantage of you.

you can hold them in the palm of your hand.

they don't mind when you talk to other guys.

21

Telephones Are Better Than Men Because...

you can open them up to see what they are made of.

you can turn them on at work.

they don't expect anything from you after the first date.

Telephones Are Better Than Men Because...

they don't schedule their lives around the World Series.

Telephones Are Better Than Men Because...

I KNOW YOU KNOW WHAT YOU THOUGHT YOU SAID I SAID, BUT WHAT I REALLY SAID WASN'T WHAT YOU THOUGHT I SAID, BUT WHAT I MEANT TO SAY WASN'T WHAT I SAID YOU SAID I SAID. Y'KNOW WHAT I'M SAYIN'?

they don't have problems communicating.

24

Telephones Are Better Than Men Because...

they never "forget" to ring.

you can always recharge their battery packs.

you can program them to remember phone numbers.

Telephones Are Better Than Men Because...

they don't tailgate.

Telephones Are Better Than Men Because...

you know exactly what to expect
when you touch certain spots.

they don't make you worry about your breath.

they beep when their batteries are low.

Telephones Are Better Than Men Because...

you don't have to take care of them when they're sick.

Telephones Are Better Than Men Because...

some are portable.

you and your friend can use one at the same time.

you can leave them all night in your car or purse.

Telephones Are Better Than Men Because...

they always welcome your mother's voice.

short ones or tall ones can be equally attractive.

you can get on one as soon as you get off another.

Telephones Are Better Than Men Because...

they have more memory.

Telephones Are Better Than Men Because...

they don't use stupid pick-up lines.

Telephones Are Better Than Men Because...

they work even if they are lying around the house.

the only place you can't play with one is in the library.

they don't send mixed messages.

Telephones Are Better Than Men Because ...

you can get the same one your neighbor has.

Telephones Are Better Than Men Because...

they never leave crumbs in the bed.

they don't use your toothbrush.

they never leave a ring in the tub.

Telephones Are Better Than Men Because...

they don't get bent out of shape if there are other phones
in the house.

they don't need more space.

they don't come on to your sister.

Telephones Are Better Than Men Because...

they don't have wandering eyes.

Telephones Are Better Than Men Because...

you can buy ones with bigger attachments.

Telephones Are Better Than Men Because...

you don't have to wait until halftime to talk.

they don't expect you to have little phones.

they never outgrow you.

Telephones Are Better Than Men Because...

they don't ask you to put them through college.

they don't call you by the wrong name.

they never readjust your car seat.

Telephones Are Better Than Men Because...

they don't criticize your singing.

Telephones Are Better Than Men Because...

they never get lost.

Telephones Are Better Than Men Because...

they don't expect you to change your name.

you can play with them morning, noon, and night.

it's easy to get a new one.

Telephones Are Better Than Men Because...

they can — and will — take you around the world.

Telephones Are Better Than Men Because ...

you don't have to make them take a blood test
before you use them.

they don't fall asleep while you are using them.

you can trust them.

Telephones Are Better Than Men Because...

you can keep them on a short cord
and they don't complain.

Telephones Are Better Than Men Because...

they don't jump up to leave right after you've used them.

you can get a good used one for practically nothing.

they don't talk back.

Telephones Are Better Than Men Because ...

the newer ones come with lots of options.

they're always responsive.

you can fool around with them in any number of positions.

Telephones Are Better Than Men Because...

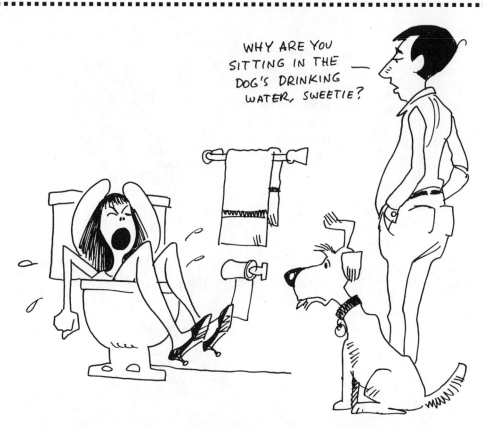

they don't leave the seat up.

Telephones Are Better Than Men Because ...

they don't lie.

Telephones Are Better Than Men Because...

they come with a warranty.

you can find the one you want in a catalog.

they are always there for you.

Telephones Are Better Than Men Because...

you don't have to worry about what they wear.

Telephones Are Better Than Men Because...

you can count on them to operate according to the manual.

they don't mind spending time with you.

they don't complain about being used, abused, or refused.

Telephones Are Better Than Men Because...

they don't leave dishes piled up in the sink.

you can just pull one right out of your purse.

you can always disconnect them when you need peace and quiet.

Telephones Are Better Than Men Because...

they're comfortable with your new piece of furniture.

Telephones Are Better Than Men Because...

they don't malfunction at the word "commitment."

Telephones Are Better Than Men Because...

you can put them on a restaurant table and use them in front of 100 people.

they never lock their keys in the car.

they don't sweat.

57

Telephones Are Better Than Men Because...

**they don't eat all your food,
even if they sit in the kitchen.**

Telephones Are Better Than Men Because...

you can swap your old model in.

they don't spit in public.

you always know where they are.

Telephones Are Better Than Men Because...

they never say, "Was it good for you?"

they know how to listen without interrupting.

you don't have to wax your legs before going out with them.

Telephones Are Better Than Men Because...

they never try to find themselves.

Telephones Are Better Than Men Because...

you don't have to deal with their side of the family.

they don't play golf.

you don't have to wait for them to "warm up."

Telephones Are Better Than Men Because...

they're easy to drop.

Telephones Are Better Than Men Because...

they're good in bed.

Telephones Are Better Than Men Because...

you can try one out in the store.

they'll never complain about having to use a condom.

they get the message.

65

Telephones Are Better Than Men Because...

they don't take up your side of the bed.

you can even use one in the bathtub.

there are no awkward first moments.

Telephones Are Better Than Men Because...

they don't leave you for a younger woman.

Telephones Are Better Than Men Because...

they don't get you pregnant.

Telephones Are Better Than Men Because...

you can have one in the car with you all day
and never hear a word about your driving.

you can find a good one no matter where you are.

they never snore.

Telephones Are Better Than Men Because...

they don't burp.

Telephones Are Better Than Men Because...

they give you more than one ring.

they can last a long time.

they don't flirt with your friends.

Telephones Are Better Than Men Because...

size really *doesn't* matter.

Telephones Are Better Than Men Because...

they couldn't care less about your body.

you use them — they never use you.

they sit patiently, no matter how long it takes
you to get ready to go out.

Telephones Are Better Than Men Because...

they don't talk to your chest instead of your eyes.

Telephones Are Better Than Men Because...

they don't have hairy backs.

it's always easy to say goodbye.

Karen Rostoker-Gruber is also the author of *Remote Controls Are Better Than Women Because . . .* and *The Unofficial College Survival Guide.* She and her husband live in Bridgewater, New Jersey.